SPECKS

A One-Act Play by
Rob Shimko

Samuel French, Inc.

 printed on recycled paper

SPECKS

A One-Act Play by
Rob Shimko

Winner of the
1998 Michael Kanin Short Play Award
given by the Kennedy Center

SAMUEL FRENCH, INC.
45 WEST 25TH STREET   NEW YORK 10010
7623 SUNSET BOULEVARD HOLLYWOOD 90046
LONDON   TORONTO

Copyright © 1999 by Rob Shimko

ALL RIGHTS RESERVED

CAUTION: Professionals and amateurs are hereby warned that SPECKS is subject to a royalty. It is fully protected under the copyright laws of the United States of America, the British Commonwealth, including Canada, and all other countries of the Copyright Union. All rights, including professional, amateur, motion pictures, recitation, lecturing, public reading, radio broadcasting, television, and the rights of translation into foreign languages are strictly reserved. In its present form the play is dedicated to the reading public only.

The amateur live stage performance rights to SPECKS are controlled exclusively by Samuel French, Inc. and royalty arrangements and licenses must be secured well in advance of presentation. PLEASE NOTE that amateur royalty fees are set upon application in accordance with your producing circumstances. When applying for a royalty quotation and license please give us the number of performances intended, dates of production, your seating capacity and admission fee. Royalties are payable one week before the opening performance of the play to Samuel French, Inc., at 45 W. 25th Street, New York, NY 10010; or at 7623 Sunset Blvd., Hollywood, CA 90046, or to Samuel French (Canada), Ltd.,100 Lombard Street, Toronto, Ontario, Canada M5C 1M3.

Royalty of the required amount must be paid whether the play is presented for charity or gain and whether or not admission is charged.

Stock royalty quoted on application to Samuel French, Inc.

For all other rights than those stipulated above, apply to Samuel French, Inc. 45 West 25th Street, New York, NY 10010.

Particular emphasis is laid on the question of amateur or professional readings, permission and terms for which must be secured in writing from Samuel French, Inc.

Copying from this book in whole or in part is strictly forbidden by law, and the right of performance is not transferable.

Whenever the play is produced the following notice must appear on all programs, printing and advertising for the play: "Produced by special arrangement with Samuel French, Inc."

Due authorship credit must be given on all programs, printing and advertising for the play.

ISBN 0 573 62663 4   Printed in the U.S.A.   # 21436

No one shall commit or authorize any act or omission by which the copyright of, or the right to copyright, this play may be impaired.

No one shall make any changes in this play for the purpose of production.

Publication of this play does not imply availability for performance. Both amateurs and professionals considering a production are *strongly* advised in their own interests to apply to Samuel French, Inc., for written permission before starting rehearsals, advertising, or booking a theater.

No part of this book may be reproduced, stored in a retrieval system, or transmitted in any form, by any means, now known or yet to be invented, including mechanical, electronic, photocopying, recording, videotaping, or otherwise, without the prior written permission of the publisher.

IMPORTANT BILLING AND CREDIT REQUIREMENTS

All producers of SPECKS *must* give credit to the Author of the Play in all programs distributed in connection with performances of the Play and in all instances in which the title of the Play appears for purposes of advertising, publicizing or otherwise exploiting the Play and/or a production. The name of the Author *must* also appear on a separate line, on which no other name appears, immediately following the title, and *must* appear in size of type not less than fifty percent the size of the title type.

SPECKS was first performaed at Hartwick College in Oneonta, NY on November 9, 1997. It was directed and designed by Rob Shimko. The cast was as follows:

Berta	Aimee Stopper
Jenner	William C. Desmarais
Molly	Sara Jean McIlvain
Paul	J.P. Luckenbach

SPECKS was later performed in the lab theater of the Kennedy Center in Washington, D.C. on April 30, 1998. It was directed by Rob Shimko and Robert Bresnick and designed by Rob Shimko and Ken Golden. The cast was as follows:

Berta	Kelly Oxton
Jenner	William C. Desmarais
Molly	Sara Jean McIlvain
Paul	J.P. Luckenbach

CHARACTERS

BERTA, a woman about fifty.

JENNER, a man in his forties.

MOLLY, a woman in her late twenties;
attractive but worn out.

PAUL, a man of about thirty;
handsome and well-dressed.

SPECKS

(A diner. New Year's Eve. A large picture window with the words "Tom 'n' Molly's Diner" painted on it stage left. Below the window, an empty booth. Downstage left, next to the window, a door leading outside. BERTA sits at a table, downstage center. Upstage center, along the back wall, are a juke box, a pay phone, and a coat rack holding BERTA and JENNER's coats. JENNER sits at the lunch counter, stage right. Behind the counter are shelves stocked with dishes and other diner ephemera. There are a few shabby Christmas decorations on the walls. Upstage right is a doorway leading to the kitchen. JENNER is eating soup. BERTA is eating french fries and alternately reading a tabloid and watching JENNER.)

BERTA. Jenner ... Jenner ... Jenner!
JENNER. What?
BERTA. Make sure to tell her the soup is good.
JENNER. What?
BERTA. When Molly comes out make sure to tell her how much you're enjoying your soup. It'll make her feel good. She's always worried about everything, the poor baby, ever since ... well, you know. And this time of year it's especially hard to be on your own. It's for the best, though. I never thought he was right for her. I was glad to see him go. Anyway, remember to say something nice about the soup.

JENNER. I would have anyway. *(He takes a bite of soup then turns to face her.)* How did you know I was eating soup?

BERTA. Well ... I watched you.

JENNER. Is that what you do?

BERTA. Every now and then I glance at you, yes. Don't be flattered. I'm just observant. *(Pause.)* Is the soup really any good?

JENNER. Yes.

BERTA. Good. *(Pause.)* What kind is it?

JENNER. Don't you know?

BERTA. Well, yes.

JENNER. Then what kind is it? You tell me what kind it is.

BERTA. Why? I mean ...

JENNER. ... Say what kind it is. You know, don't you? So say what kind it is.

BERTA. Jenner, I was just making conversation, I don't ...

JENNER. ... Tell me what kind of soup I'm eating.

BERTA. What's wrong with you?

JENNER. Don't change the subject. Just tell me what you saw me eating.

BERTA. Okay, it's ...

JENNER. ... It's not mushroom, is it?

BERTA. What? No.

JENNER. That's right. You'll never see me order mushroom soup. Mushroom soup makes me puke.

BERTA. I'm sorry.

JENNER. That's all right ... And don't think that we're done with this, either. You still haven't told me what kind of soup I'm eating.

BERTA. Why do you need me to tell you? You already know.

JENNER. Because I told you to tell me! Because you're always bothering me about nothing. You sit there and twitter at me every night, all night long. If I'm sitting here quietly, it's usually because I'm thinking about something, but you don't care about that. You want to make small talk endlessly, no matter what I'm doing. *You* want to know what's wrong with me? *That's* what's wrong with me. You know what I'm eating but you ask me anyway. So you tell *me* what kind of soup I'm eating.

BERTA. Fine! It's tomato soup. It's tomato soup, and I won't be nice to you ever again.

JENNER. You see? That wasn't so hard.

(JENNER turns back to his soup then realizes something. He turns back to BERTA and stares at her until she looks up.)

BERTA. What?
JENNER. Say it again.
BERTA. Oh, Jesus.
JENNER. *(Coaxing, patronizing.)* Say it again.
BERTA. It's tomato soup.
JENNER. Wrong! *(Joyous.)* Wrong! It is *not* tomato soup. It's tomato *rice*. I can't believe you said tomato. There's a lesson for you about being precise. Is there anything else you want to ask me?

BERTA. Not right now.

JENNER. Okay. *(Mockingly, to himself.)* It's tomato, Jenner. Ha Ha.

(JENNER turns back to his soup. MOLLY emerges from the kitchen and sets a plate down in front of him.)

MOLLY. Here you go. One club sandwich, extra bacon, no mayo. How's the soup?

JENNER. Very good.

MOLLY. Good. *(She watches as he takes a bit of the sandwich.)* How's the sandwich? *(JENNER chews rapidly for a long time.)* Sorry.

JENNER. *(Swallowing.)* That's okay. It's good, too.

MOLLY. Good. *(Under her breath.)* Good Good Good.

JENNER. *(Sheepishly.)* Everything's been real good since, uh, since Tom ... left. You're doing a real good job, Molly. I always liked your cooking better, anyway.

MOLLY. You're sweet. I'm glad you like it. You *are* my second best customer.

JENNER. That's, uh, that's good to know. I mean I'm glad that you think, um, think of me enough to mention it. *(Quietly, so BERTA can't hear.)* Molly, can I ask you something? It's been awhile since you've been on your own, and I was wondering, would you ...

BERTA. ... Molly, honey, come her.

MOLLY. Hold on. What is it you want to ask me, Jenner?

JENNER. Never mind.

MOLLY. Are you sure?

JENNER. Yeah, it'll keep.

MOLLY. Well ... okay.

(MOLLY crosses to table.)

BERTA. What was it you were going to ask Molly, Jenner?

JENNER. *(Embarrassed.)* Never mind!

BERTA. I just wanted to tell you, you know what tonight is, don't you?

MOLLY. Yes, Mom, I know. But it doesn't mean anything. It's just another night. It's not going to upset me. I don't need to kiss someone at midnight or anything like that. It's all right. The only excitement I need is throwing out the old calendar and putting up the new one you gave me, thank you again.

BERTA. Oh, you're welcome, sweetheart, but don't talk like that. You need to have some fun. You're going to work yourself to death. They're having a party in the building across the street again this year. I've seen at least sixty people go in.

They're going to wake the Devil tonight.

MOLLY. Terrific.

BERTA. I never get invited to New Year's Eve parties anymore. I used to be much more social. When I lived in Buffalo with your Aunt Lucy we used to have a corker of a party every New Year's Eve. At midnight, everyone would go up to the roof of our apartment building and slide around in the snow and the ice. Once year I almost fell over the side, but your father caught me. He wasn't your father then—I hardly knew him—but he caught me anyway. He used to say that was what he like most about me: I knew how to enjoy myself. I used to do this one thing where I would stand in the middle of the room and put a coffee cup on my head and then fill it up. One time I got coffee on my head and the cup fell on the floor. Everybody laughed—a lot more than when I filled it up with no problem. That's what people like to see. Everybody laughed really hard and I laughed too. It was a good party. *(Beat.)* It changes though—what you think of as fun, I mean. I sure as hell wouldn't want to slide around in the snow anymore. Things calmed down when I had you. And now I never get invited to parties at all. I thought maybe I'd do something about that. I thought maybe I'd throw my own party.

MOLLY. Really, when?

BERTA. I thought maybe tonight.

MOLLY. *(Wary.)* At home?

BERTA. Well, no. I mean it's only about *(Looking at her watch.)* forty minutes till midnight. If I were throwing a party there I wouldn't be here would I? No, I ... I thought maybe I could have it here. If you don't mind, I mean. It'll be so much fun. We can play games and count down to midnight and make resolutions together. Do you mind?

MOLLY. That depends on who's coming.

BERTA. Oh, well, that's just you, me, and Jenner: the usual suspects. *(Announcing.)* Round up the usual suspects—for a party! *(BERTA chuckles to herself. MOLLY opens her mouth to talk, but BERTA cuts her off.)* Hold on a second. *(BERTA digs around in her purse and pulls out three paper party hats and toy horns.)* Here, Molly. Put the hat on now but don't blow the horn until midnight, okay? *(MOLLY looks at them but does not take them. She looks embarrassed.)* I'll see if Jenner wants a hat. *(Shouting across the diner.)* Jenner, do you want a party hat? We're having a party. Jenner! I said, 'do you want a party hat?!'

JENNER. No.

BERTA. But ...

JENNER. ... No.

BERTA. Then what are you going to do tonight? Are you just going to sit there? Are you going to make another damn castle tonight?

JENNER. It's not a castle.

BERTA. Tower. Sorry. They're towers. But not tonight though, please. You'll miss all the fun. *(BERTA puts on her party hat. To MOLLY.)* Okay, take yours and just leave his on the counter next to him.

MOLLY. Mom, I ... fine. *(Grudgingly, she puts on her party hat.)* Do you want any coffee or anything? I'm going to start a new pot.

BERTA. Okay, but only if you would have made it anyway. *(MOLLY starts toward the kitchen but BERTA stops her.)* and Honey? Happy New Year's.

(MOLLY exits stage left. On her way she places a party hat and horn on the counter next to JENNER. BERTA picks at her food for a little then takes a drink from her water glass. She puts the glass down and notices something in it.)

BERTA. (Cont.) Jenner. *(JENNER looks up from eating, takes in a big breath and slowly lets it out.)* Jenner, look at this.

JENNER. What?

BERTA. Look at this.
JENNER. No.
BERTA. Come on.
JENNER. I'm eating!

(Pause. BERTA looks intently at her water glass.)

BERTA. There's a bug in my water, Jenner. And not just floating in the water, it's in the ice. Frozen in the ice. It's like that joke where you get a fake ice cube with a fly in it. *(She sticks her finger in the glass to feel the ice cube.)* But this isn't fake. And it's not a very funny joke—to put a fly in someone's drink. *(As she continues examining.)* But it's not really a fly, Jenner. It's smaller than a fly. It's like a gnat. Actually, all I can really tell is that it's a speck of something. Just a little black speck of something frozen in my ice.

JENNER. There are little black specks everywhere.

BERTA. Well, yes, Jenner, of course, but in my drink there shouldn't be. *(Pause.)* Should I tell Molly?

JENNER. Tell her what?

BERTA. About the fly.

JENNER. You said it was a speck. I wish you would keep your story straight.

BERTA. *(Resolving.)* I won't tell her. I suppose it's okay to drink as long as whatever it is stays frozen in the ice. I mean, it's not touching anything. Except I've been sticking my fingers in it so much that now there's probably something else in it. I need new water. *(Pause. JENNER eats. BERTA starts looking at and then rubbing her right arm.)* My arm hurts, Jenner.

JENNER. *(Very annoyed.)* Yes?

BERTA. Yes. It's hurt all night. It's numb.

JENNER. Then it doesn't hurt.

BERTA. What do you mean it doesn't hurt? How would you know? It's my arm and it hurts.

JENNER. You said it was numb. If it's numb you can't feel anything so it can't hurt.

BERTA. *(Authoritative.)* A numb arm can signal a heart attack, Jenner.

JENNER. Are you having a heart attack, Berta?

BERTA. Well ... no ... probably not. But would it kill you to act concerned? To just take a little notice of things now and then? It would teach you a lot. It would open your eyes. You'd learn to have consideration for others. I watch everything that goes on in here and it's taught me quite a bit about human beings, I can tell you. Yes, sir. You'd be amazed by the things I know. Truly amazed.

JENNER. Are you sure it's not a heart attack?
BERTA. Yes!

(MOLLY enters. BERTA sees her and knocks over her water glass.)

BERTA. Oops. Oh, Lord. Sweetheart I made a mess. I'm sorry.

(MOLLY crosses to BERTA and wipes up the mess.)

MOLLY. Don't worry about it. I'll get you some new water.

(MOLLY exits into the kitchen.)

BERTA. You see that? I'm a genius, Jenner.

(MOLLY returns with a pitcher and fills BERTA's glass.)

MOLLY. Coffee'll be ready soon.
BERTA. Thanks. Sorry again.
MOLLY. It's all right.

(MOLLY exits. JENNER, who has finished his meal, has started to methodically organize his dishes and silverware. Eventually, he will begin to stack them one on top of another, creating a large tower.)

BERTA. Jenner, don't start that tonight.
JENNER. I can't help it. I want to.
BERTA. You want to keep your head buried in the sand, that's what you want. But not tonight. Please. It's New Year's Eve. Let's have some fun, just you and me. I'll play some music. *(She gets up and walks to the juke box and selects a fifties ballad. She listens until the first line of the song.)* Isn't that nice? *(She sways with the music as she walks over to JENNER and dances slowly behind him.)* Do you want to dance with me, Jenner?
JENNER. No.
BERTA. Why not?
JENNER. I don't feel like it.
BERTA. There was a time when you would have been dying to.
JENNER. Oh?
BERTA. *(Slightly defensive.)* Yes. I was very pretty, and all the boys lined up to dance with me. *(Calmer, becoming seductive, still swaying.)* When was the last time you danced?
JENNER. Please don't start this.
BERTA. What were you going to ask my Molly, Jenner?
JENNER. Nothing, I ...
BERTA. Was it a question about the menu? I bet it wasn't.
JENNER. Look, Berta, I ...
BERTA. ... Was it something dirty, Jenner? Something you shouldn't ask a vulnerable girl?
JENNER. No, I was just going to ... never mind.
BERTA. She's still confused about Tom. She's fragile, you know. But I'm not. No, I'm not fragile at all. Dance with me, Jenner. Stand up and put your hand on my hip.

JENNER. Berta, I ...

BERTA. ... What were you going to say to my daughter, Jenner? Tell me. Say it to me. Say it to *me*. Tell me what it is that you want.

JENNER. Don't do this.

BERTA. Oh, but don't you know I have to. It's New Year's Eve. *(Putting her hands on his knees.)* Now tell me.

JENNER. I can't tell you, so stop it! I ... I want ... *(Calming down.)* I want to be left alone.

(The door opens and in walks PAUL. Ideally, this will coincide with the final line of the song. He looks at BERTA and JENNER and they look at him. PAUL takes his coat off and hangs it up.)

BERTA. Hello. I'm Berta. Happy New Year's. *(Pause.)* We're having a party, sort of. Do you want a hat?

PAUL. No thanks.

(BERTA moves to the booth. PAUL sits at the center table, ignoring BERTA's place setting.)

BERTA. *(Annoyed, grabbing her horn off the table.)* How about a horn?

PAUL. No thanks.

BERTA. That's Jenner. He's sort of shy if you don't know him. He said he didn't want a hat either. *(To JENNER.)* But it's there if you change your mind.

(MOLLY emerges from the kitchen with a pot of coffee. She notices PAUL and they look at each other. She is a little confused about the new seating arrangements. Then she remembers her hat and takes it off. She crosses to BERTA and fills her cup.)

MOLLY. Here you go.

(MOLLY moves to PAUL.)

MOLLY. What can I get for you?
PAUL. Just coffee for now, thanks. *(MOLLY fills his cup.)* I see you took off your hat.
MOLLY. I'm not feeling all that festive.
PAUL. I understand.
MOLLY. Have you been out tonight?
PAUL. Yes.
MOLLY. Let me guess, you were across the street, right?
PAUL. I was actually. You know that tonight was the sixth year in a row that I went to that same goddamn New Year's Eve party? Every year my friends get very excited for it. Everyone dresses up, the drinks are free, it's a beautiful apartment. Have you ever been in that building? It's a nice building.
MOLLY. Yeah. I used to know someone who lived there. He moved, though.
PAUL. Which floor?
MOLLY. Third.
PAUL. The party's on the fourth.
MOLLY. You left before midnight.
PAUL. True.
MOLLY. Why?
PAUL. I just felt like it. It's supposed to be this great party and everyone's supposed to have a good time, but I've been going for six years and I've never enjoyed it once. My friends keep telling me that I should loosen up and have some fun.
MOLLY. Why can't you? It sounds like an all right party.
PAUL. You're right, it does. I mean, even *I* think I should be having a good time. But look at this. *(PAUL raises his leg and rests it on the chair to his right with his foot sticking out.)* You see this shoe? It looks like a nice shoe, right? My best pair—Italian leather, handmade, beautiful. But what you can't

see is that it pinches my toes like a son of a bitch. That party's the same way. You can't see the pinch, but it's there. Understand?

MOLLY. I think so. Do you want something to eat?

PAUL. Not yet. Can I just sit here for a little bit?

MOLLY. Sure. My mother may start badgering you to put on a hat, though. *She's* not sour on parties.

BERTA. I'm not going to badger anybody.

MOLLY. Okay, Mom.

(BERTA momentarily turns her attention to her coffee.)

PAUL. She's your mother?

MOLLY. Yeah. She comes in at night to keep me company.

PAUL. You need company?

MOLLY. Not really. She says I work too hard.

PAUL. Do you work too hard?

MOLLY. Maybe.

PAUL. Are you the "Molly" from the sign?

MOLLY. Yeah.

PAUL. Where's the "Tom" from the sign?

MOLLY. The "Tom" from the sign is a long story.

PAUL. Oh ... sorry.

MOLLY. It's all right. *(Pause.)* I almost sold the place, but I got scared about what I would do next. It's not even worth that much. We bought it for next to nothing. At the very least I should get around to scraping his name off the window.

PAUL. But you'd get out if you could?

MOLLY. Get out of?

PAUL. The diner business.

MOLLY. I don't know. You want to make me an offer?

PAUL. No, I don't suppose so. You do the cooking too?

MOLLY. We have a cook and another waitress during the day, but it's just me at night. We don't get much night trade outside the regulars.

PAUL. What are you doing right now?
MOLLY. Running my diner.
PAUL. Yes, but is there anything pressing—waffles burning in the back, something like that—or can you sit for a minute?
MOLLY. I don't burn waffles, and yes, I can sit. *(She takes the seat next to PAUL's right.)* What's on your mind?

(PAUL takes out a cigarette and searches for a lighter.)

PAUL. Got a light? I must have left mine somewhere.
MOLLY. No. I'm sorry.
PAUL. That's all right. *(He twists the cigarette around in his fingers for a moment then puts it away.)* I've been rolling some things over in my head tonight. I was trying to tell this girl about something at the party, but she wasn't interested. That's about when I left.
MOLLY. What were you trying to say?
PAUL. I was thinking about something that happened to me not too long ago. It was stupid. I was trying to explain ... You sure you want to hear this?
MOLLY. Why not?
PAUL. All right, well, this all happened about six months ago, in the summer. I was driving, and I had this ... memory. It was one of those long drives when you get a little crazy and your mind starts to wander, you know. Well, when I was a teenager, I used to read my dad's *USA Today* with my cereal before school, and one day I read this article about a guy who was a bowler. He bowled every weekend, or whatever, and he really liked it, and he was pretty good, but he had never bowled a three hundred, which is a perfect game.
MOLLY. I know.

(PAUL smiles at her.)

PAUL. So his wife, for his birthday, buys him this new bowling ball. And lo and behold, the first time he goes out and uses it, he bowls a perfect game. The guy, of course, can't believe it. He starts shouting and jumping up and down and shit. So everyone in the bowling alley sort of gathers around him and they're cheering for him and he's cheering and it's the best moment of his life. Then, in the middle of all of this cheering—Bang! He dies of a heart attack. Right there. Right in the middle of everyone who was cheering for him. The closest thing I can imagine is dying while you're having sex—one minute you feel everything ... and the next ... nothing. Anyway, it was such a crazy story that it made it into *USA Today*. They put a picture of the guy next to the article, and I'll tell you, in the picture he looked really surprised. I don't think they took it after he bowled the perfect game, it was probably just a family snapshot, so I figure he just looked surprised all the time. Well, since I had a sick sense of humor like every teenager, I cut it out and put it on my wall. I probably still have it somewhere.

MOLLY. That's quite a story.

PAUL. Oh, that's not the story. That's just the introduction. That's just what I was thinking about while I was driving that day. What happened in the car is the story. It's probably because of this story that I'm here with you now instead of getting quietly toasted at that damn party. So anyway, I'm going down the highway thinking about this guy and how he never saw it coming, and I start thinking about when I'm going to die. I mean it sounds weird, but we all do it, right? You've got to think about something on a long drive. Well, as I'm thinking this, I start to get very uncomfortable in the car, like I could be moving toward some terrible fate and not even know it. And it's worse because whenever I'm in the car I'm always trying to make good time and I look at the speedometer and the clock, a lot. Well, I've found that if you do that enough, that you can sort of feel yourself moving through time as you as you move down the road. Do you get what I mean?

MOLLY. Yeah, I do that too.

PAUL. So anyway, I've managed to make myself real nervous as I'm driving. It's how I suppose it would feel if your horoscope told you not to go on that trip you were planning, and you went anyway, but the whole time you felt like you were doing something that you shouldn't be and sooner or later you were going to pay for it. I felt crazy for making myself worry like that, but no matter how much you want to stop worrying about it you can't because there it is. You try to trick yourself into thinking about something else, but it always comes back. So then, because I can't stop thinking about dying, I pick out this big road sign as far away as I can see, and I imagine that all the time I have left in the world is the time between right now and when I get to the sign. And I get more and more afraid of what's going to happen as I get closer to the sign. Everything starts to slow down and get really clear. The announcer on the radio was the funniest thing because he's going on about where the President's going to be this weekend or something, and, I mean, what's that going to do for me now, right? I'm about to die! I'm sweating and the sign is getting closer and closer and I can't do anything about it. It's time to check out, and who can argue with that? Not me ... So as I finally pass the sign, I close my eyes, and I tell you I feel dead. And it really wasn't so bad. It's warm. It's warm because the sun's shining on my face, but I didn't realize that at the time. I'm driving with my eyes closed and it feels just wonderful. I feel very warm and relaxed, and I can feel the steering wheel in my hands, but I can't see anything or hear anything—the radio just blocked itself out. I'm completely at peace and flying down the road, probably with a big stupid grin on my face. The thing is, though, that I feel so, I don't know, I guess the best word is "settled." I feel so settled that I can't open my eyes again. I'm roaring down the highway at seventy, eighty miles an hour and I can't open my eyes! I'm trying and trying but I just can't because deep down I don't want to. I'm just going to keep my eyes closed and keep going.

MOLLY. So, what happened?

PAUL. I ran off the road! The car rolled over three times. I should have been killed, but I ended up with just a broken arm and some "minor cuts and bruises". They had to use the jaws of life to get me out.

MOLLY. Jesus. You were lucky.

PAUL. That's what all my friends said, that it was a miracle that I survived at all. But do you know what? Part of me wishes I could have gone right then, because at least I was ready. I had resigned myself to the fact that I was going to die. When I do go, I doubt I'll have that peace of mind. *(Silence. Everyone looks at PAUL.)* Sorry, maybe I shouldn't have ...

MOLLY. ... Oh, no. No. It's all right. You don't have to explain. (Pause.) Do you want to order something now?

PAUL. Yes.

MOLLY. What do you want?

PAUL. *(Looking at menu.)* How do you make the reuben sandwich?

MOLLY. With pastrami, not corned beef.

PAUL. That's good. Pastrami is better, but I meant how do you prepare it?

MOLLY. I put pastrami, sauerkraut, Swiss cheese and Russian dressing on rye bread and fry it. That's how it's done, isn't it?

PAUL. Yes, but there's more to it than that if you want to do it right. For instance, what kind of pastrami do you use?

MOLLY. Plain old pastrami.

PAUL. You see, what you want is black pastrami, it's more peppery. It tastes a little like beef jerky.

MOLLY. I could put pepper on it if you want.

PAUL. No, that's all right, just remember what I tell you for the future. Okay, so the first thing you want to do is you want to start the sauerkraut and the pastrami cooking first.

Just put them on the grill and let them heat up. The thing doesn't cook right if you don't heat up the inside first. While that's going, you want to make your Russian dressing.

MOLLY. I already have Russian dressing.

PAUL. Yes and it comes in a big plastic jug and it tastes like vinegar and glue. You make your Russian dressing by mixing mayonnaise with chili sauce and horseradish. Do you have all that?

MOLLY. Usually, I'll have to look. You really have this down to a science.

PAUL. It's the only thing I know how to make. So your meat and your sauerkraut are almost done. Now you want to butter two pieces of hard Jewish rye bread. Put the bottom piece on the grill and put your meat, kraut, dressing, and cheese on in that order. The meat and the cheese keep the bread from getting soggy. Then just grill it how you usually would.

MOLLY. So that's what you want?

PAUL. That's what I want.

(MOLLY stands.)

MOLLY. You're a demanding guy. I'll do my best.

PAUL. That's fine. *(MOLLY starts to exit.)* One thing before you go. What do you think they would have done with the bowling ball? I mean, it seems to me like the thing was cursed. I wonder where it ended up. Well, something to think about while you're making the sandwich.

(MOLLY exits into the kitchen. PAUL sits thinking. He looks at his watch and then out the window intently for a moment. He watches JENNER curiously then looks at BERTA.)

PAUL. (Cont.) Come here, Berta. I want to talk to you.
BERTA. You want to talk to me?
PAUL. Yes. *(Indicating the chair to his left.)* Come sit here.

(BERTA gets up and walks over to PAUL's table.)

    BERTA. Here?
    PAUL. Yes.

(They sit in silence, BERTA is a little nervous. PAUL just looks at her.)

    BERTA. I heard that story you told about the car accident. You should be careful. A car can be so dangerous.
    PAUL. You're right.
    BERTA. I don't drive. I walk everywhere. It's good for your heart, you know.
    PAUL. *(Looking around.)* It's not much of a party.
    BERTA. No. It's hard to get people to have fun.
    PAUL. Yeah, I know all about that. But I have a feeling about tonight. Tonight's not over yet, is it?
    BERTA. No.
    PAUL. Not even close. There's still plenty of fun to be had. We're going to raise the roof.
    BERTA. We're gonna wake the Devil.
    PAUL. Well said.

(Pause.)

    BERTA. What should we do?
    PAUL. We'll wait, something will happen.
    BERTA. Yes. *(Pause.)* What?
    PAUL. Does your arm hurt, Berta? I've seen you rubbing it.
    BERTA. It ... hurts ... yes.
    PAUL. Would you like me to rub it?
    BERTA. Would you?
    PAUL. Sure.
    BERTA. I can't remember the last time I got a massage.

(PAUL rubs BERTA's arm sensuously.)

PAUL. How does that feel?
BERTA. Good. Why are you doing this?
PAUL. You looked like you could use it.
BERTA. Thank you. *(Pause.)* It's not fair that I should have to put up with so much.
PAUL. What do you mean?
BERTA. I do so much for everyone, and no one ever does for me. I sit in the corner and get ignored. I try to show them a good time and they resent it. That feels good, right there.
PAUL. Do you know why bad things happen to good people, Berta? Because they're so afraid that bad things will happen to them. It's fear that makes bad things happen. You should stop being afraid and let something good happen to you.
BERTA. I'm not afraid. What's going to happen tonight? You said something would happen tonight.

(PAUL starts massaging BERTA's hand.)

PAUL. How does that feel? Most people neglect the hands when they give a massage. You have a lot of tension in your fingers.
BERTA. I do?
PAUL. Yes, you do. You have knots. You have to press hard to work knots out. You have to crush them, otherwise they just slide around under your skin.
BERTA. That ... hurts. Ow! That hurts!
PAUL. Oh, I'm sorry.
BERTA. That's okay, but you can stop now.

(BERTA stands up.)

PAUL. I am sorry.

(PAUL stands up and moves toward BERTA.)

BERTA. *(Backing away slightly.)* It's all right.

(PAUL looks over at JENNER. By now JENNER's tower is quite large, incorporating clean dishes taken from the place setting next to him.)

PAUL. *(Softly, so JENNER can't hear.)* What is he doing?

BERTA. He does that almost every night. He won't tell me why. I used to think it was kind of interesting. He's an odd duck.

PAUL. Do you think he'd mind if I asked him about it?

BERTA. He likes to be left alone.

PAUL. But it couldn't hurt to just ask.

BERTA. I don't know. Maybe you'd better ...

(PAUL walks over to JENNER. BERTA returns to the booth. PAUL stands behind JENNER and watches him tinker with his construction.)

PAUL. Excuse me. *(Pause.)* Excuse me.

JENNER. What do you want?

PAUL. I was just wondering what you were doing. With the dishes, I mean.

JENNER. I'd think that you'd be able to figure that out without asking.

PAUL. That's true. What I meant to say is why are you doing it?

JENNER. It occurred to me to do it, that's all. I like to see things in order.

PAUL. This is order, everything stacked up like this?

JENNER. That's how I see it, yes. A place for everything and everything in it's place.

PAUL But is everything in its proper place? Maybe that's

what you should ask yourself. I hear you do this every night.

JENNER. *(Turning sharply on BERTA.)* Don't talk about me behind my back!

PAUL. No. It's my fault. I asked her about you. I was curious. I'm sorry. *(Pause.)* Well, you sure have it made here, don't you? Two good-looking women around all the time, and here you are with them all to yourself. Yes, you sure do have it made, don't you think?

JENNER. I suppose so.

PAUL. You suppose so. You hear that, Berta? Jenner says he has it made, having two beautiful women around all the time.

BERTA. You said that, Jenner?

JENNER. What are you trying to pull?

PAUL. Nothing. Nothing at all. Just making conversation.

(MOLLY enters from the kitchen, carrying PAUL's sandwich. PAUL returns to his seat.)

MOLLY. Okay, now try it and tell me what you think.

PAUL. It smells good. *(PAUL takes a bite and chews for a long time, analyzing it.)* It's very good for a beginner.

MOLLY. Really? Thanks. I wasn't sure I cooked the sauerkraut long enough.

PAUL. No, it's just fine. Everything's very nicely blended. You didn't use too much horseradish. That's important. Yes, this is a sandwich I could get used to. Would you like a bite?

MOLLY. Well, I don't usually ...

PAUL. ... I know you don't usually, but this isn't a usual night. Try it. You should at least know how it tastes.

MOLLY. Well, okay. *(She sits. PAUL hands her the sandwich and she takes a bite.)* Oh, that is good. I don't usually like them.

PAUL. Nothing else tastes like that—sour and spicy and some other things you just can't describe.

MOLLY. Sort of ... fatty.

PAUL. *(Laughing.)* That's probably it.

BERTA. I don't mean to interrupt, but it's only about ten minutes to twelve and I was hoping that we could all put on our hats and make resolutions before midnight. It's so much fun to count down to a new year.

PAUL. Yes, of course. That would be nice, but could I finish my sandwich first, please?

BERTA. Oh, yes. Go ahead. I'm sorry, I didn't mean to hurry you. I'll just amuse myself until everyone's ready.

PAUL. Thank you.

BERTA. *(To herself.)* As usual.

(Silence. BERTA looks out the window. It is apparent that she thinks she sees something out of the ordinary across the street. PAUL savors his sandwich and MOLLY watches him. They exchange a few flirtatious smiles. JENNER straightens his tower, notices the party hat that has been sitting next to him on the counter, then, after serious consideration, decides to put it on top of the tower. Finally, BERTA can stay quiet no longer.)

BERTA. Um ... I hate to interrupt again, but I think I see something across the street.

MOLLY. What, Mom?

BERTA. Well, I'm not sure, but it looks like there may be some smoke coming from ...

PAUL. ... All right, I'm done with my sandwich. Let's make some resolutions.

MOLLY. *What* did you see?

PAUL. It's probably just the reflection on the glass; it's nothing. Now let's all make our resolutions before it's too late. Berta, come away from the window. That's right. Come on, Jenner, it's time to join the party.

BERTA. But what about ...

PAUL. No buts. It's your party, you don't want to miss it, do you?
BERTA. Oh, no. That's right. I'm glad you showed up.
PAUL. So am I.

(BERTA and MOLLY join PAUL at his table. JENNER looks at them but stays put.)

BERTA. Jenner, please join us.
JENNER. I don't know. I ... no. I'm busy.

(JENNER turns back to his tower and tinkers with it.)

BERTA. Oh, well fine.
PAUL. Berta, would you like to make the first resolution?
BERTA. Oh, yes. Let me see ... I'm so excited. It makes it hard. Okay. I resolve ... um ... I resolve that in the new year I will ... I've got it! I resolve that in the new year, I will go to more parties.
MOLLY. Good, Mom. That's a good one. I resolve to make reuben sandwiches the right way.
PAUL. And I resolve to give up smoking. Jenner, are you sure you don't want to make a resolution?
MOLLY. Come on, we all did.
BERTA. My mother used to say that if you don't make a resolution, the new year may never come.
PAUL. Do you hear that, Jenner? You might not be around in the morning if you don't resolve something quick.
JENNER. Will you all leave me alone! How many times do I have to ...

(BERTA interrupts JENNER by blowing her party horn at him.)

BERTA. Oh, that's neat! *(To MOLLY.)* Isn't that neat? Molly, gets yours. *(To PAUL.)* You can have Jenner's since he doesn't want it. We can all blow them together. *(PAUL walks over to JENNER and picks up his horn. JENNER grabs it, but PAUL pulls it away from him. Then BERTA, PAUL, and MOLLY make a racket with their horns.)* You see, now it's a party. We should play a game.

PAUL. What game would you like to play, Berta? Hide and seek?

MOLLY. There's not much room in here.

BERTA. Duck Duck Goose?

PAUL. With only four? You're playing, right Jenner?

BERTA. Pin the tail on the donkey?

PAUL. That can be dangerous—walking around blind with something sharp. No. *(Flirting with BERTA.)* How about spin the bottle?

BERTA. *(Giggling.)* Oh, stop.

PAUL. I've got it: twenty questions.

BERTA. Oh yes. Yes. Yes.

MOLLY. Who will we ask?

BERTA. *(To PAUL.)* We'll ask you —go first.

PAUL. Oh, not me. Not first. Jenner why don't you go first.

JENNER. I'm not playing.

PAUL. Yes you are.

BERTA. Come on, Jenner, don't be a lump.

JENNER. No.

MOLLY. Come on, it might be fun.

(Short pause as JENNER thinks it over.)

JENNER. Well, what do I have to do?

BERTA. You think of something—a place or a famous person or something—and we have to figure out what it is by asking you twenty questions or less, and you can only answer "yes" or "no." *(To MOLLY.)* We played it when I was little. I'm a wonderful guesser.

MOLLY. Let's do a famous person first. Jenner, think of a

famous person. Got one? *(JENNER nods.)* Good.

BERTA. Is it a man?

JENNER. Yes.

BERTA. A young man?

JENNER. No.

MOLLY. An old man?

JENNER. No.

BERTA. *(To MOLLY.)* That means he's middle aged. Remember to conserve your questions Is he an actor?

JENNER. No.

MOLLY. A politician?

JENNER. No.

BERTA. Is he American?

JENNER. Yes.

PAUL. Is he fat?

JENNER. What? Uh, sort of.

PAUL. *(Snapping.)* You can't say sort of, you can only say yes or no!

JENNER. Y-y-yes, then. He's fat.

BERTA. Is he a singer?

PAUL. You know, Jenner you're getting a little hefty yourself.

BERTA. I said, "is he a singer?"

PAUL. You want to know what I think, Jenner? I think you picked yourself. Is it you Jenner?

JENNER. No. It's ... it's not.

PAUL. Are you sure? You're a middle aged American man, right? Getting a little chubby? Are you sure you haven't mistaken yourself for some big star? You do have a certain star quality, Jenner, a certain *Je-ne-sais-quois.* Do you sit at that counter every day?

JENNER. Yes.

PAUL. Do you think you'll ever be "discovered"—get that big break?

JENNER. No.

PAUL. No? So what you're saying is that you don't want anything more than this? You're a big enough star right here for these two. Berta, do you think Jenner could be a movie star?

BERTA. I think so, sure.

PAUL. See, Jenner, it's time you left the safety of this diner. It's time you took a chance. It's time for bigger and better things. What do you do for a living?

JENNER. I ... I can't answer that.

PAUL. Ah, yes. Do you work hard then?

JENNER. Yes.

PAUL. Do you make waves?

JENNER. What?

PAUL. You know, at work, do you rock the boat, cause a stir?

JENNER. No.

PAUL. Do you ever get frustrated at work?

JENNER. Yes.

PAUL. Do you ever feel like everything in the world is spinning out of control, and that you have no say in your own life?

JENNER. I don't know what you ...

PAUL. ... Yes or no!

JENNER. Yes!

PAUL. Have you ever killed anyone?

JENNER. No! What's going ...

PAUL. ... Have you ever killed anything? An animal?

JENNER. Yes. It was an accident. I hit a dog with my car.

PAUL. Of course. How did you feel? Did you feel bad?

JENNER. Yes.

PAUL. Do you feel bad now? Are you afraid?

JENNER. I ...

PAUL. *(Friendly.)* You don't have to answer. What is that you're making?

JENNER. It's ...

PAUL. ... Only yes or no! Do you do that every night?
JENNER. Yes.
PAUL. I've been watching you Jenner. I know what you're doing! I know what you're up to with those dishes! You're making a mess Jenner! Do you expect Molly to clean up your mess every night?
JENNER. No.
PAUL. *(Hitting a fever pitch.)* Then what are you going to do? What's it gonna be, Jenner? Are you gonna be a bum all your life?
JENNER. No! *(Panting.)* That's ... that's twenty.

(Silence.)

MOLLY. Well who the hell was it, anyway?
JENNER. It was Elvis.
BERTA. I knew it was a singer.
MOLLY. Elvis isn't middle-aged, Elvis is dead.
PAUL. Anyone want to play again? I've got a good one.
BERTA. *(A little afraid.)* Not now, it's almost midnight. Okay, everybody gather around. It's almost time ... twenty seconds.
PAUL. *(To MOLLY.)* You know, I hope you keep your resolution. There's nowhere around here that makes a good reuben.
MOLLY. No sweat. You just keep coming by.
BERTA. Okay, everybody count! Ten! Nine! ...

(Everyone counts down to midnight then screams "Happy New Year" with varying levels of enthusiasm. BERTA starts singing "Auld Lang Syne." PAUL takes MOLLY in his arms and they kiss. JENNER sees this and rushes over to them. He pulls PAUL away from MOLLY violently. BERTA stops singing. The sound of a fire can be heard very faintly from stage left. This sound should gradually increase in intensity until the end of the play.)

JENNER. Get away from her! What do you think you're doing?
MOLLY. Jenner, it's all right.
JENNER. It is not all right! You stay away from her!
MOLLY. Jesus, Jenner, leave him alone.
JENNER. Molly, what are you doing? How can you ... I mean ...
MOLLY. Jenner, calm down. It's okay. Nothing's wrong. Now sit back down and just try to relax.

(MOLLY leads JENNER back to his seat.)

JENNER. Molly, I just wanted ...
MOLLY. I know. I know. And I'm sorry.
BERTA. *(To PAUL.)* Maybe you shouldn't have been so mean to him during the game. That was ... I mean I never saw anything like that.
PAUL. Don't worry. I was just shaking him up a little. Everyone needs that. It's good for you. Now why don't you go sit down. *(BERTA starts toward her booth, but PAUL stops her.)* And Berta, happy new year.

(BERTA starts back toward the booth. As she gets near, she glances out the window. She sees something that shocks her and she rushes to the window.)

BERTA. Oh my God!
MOLLY. What?
BERTA. Come here! Oh my God, Molly, hurry! The building across the street! It's on fire!
PAUL. What?
BERTA. Look! Oh my God! You see, I knew I saw smoke!
PAUL. I'll call the fire department.

(PAUL goes to the pay phone and picks up the receiver but does not dial. JENNER sits with his head in his hands. MOLLY has joined BERTA at the window.)

MOLLY. God, look at it.
BERTA. Jenner, come here and see this. *(To MOLLY.)* The people are getting out, it looks like. Should we do something? Should we go over there?
PAUL. Don't go outside. Let the fire department handle it.
BERTA. I ... I guess you're right.
MOLLY. Look at it go, just eating up everything. It's spreading so fast. I'll go turn out the lights so we can see better.

(MOLLY crosses to behind the counter and turns off the lights while PAUL joins BERTA at the window. For the rest of the play, the room is lit by fire light. MOLLY notices JENNER sulking and moves to face him across the counter.)

BERTA. Do you see your friends? Are they getting out?
MOLLY. I know you were only trying to look out for me just now, but please don't be angry.
PAUL. Yes, I can see them.
MOLLY. He's the first man since Tom that's made me feel anything. The way he talks to me, it's just ... I don't know.
BERTA. Don't you want to go over there to check on them?
MOLLY. And I don't know if anything will come of it, but I don't want it to end before it even starts, so please.
PAUL. No.
JENNER. I don't know what to say.
BERTA. Why not?
MOLLY. Just don't say anything, and we'll see how this turns out.
PAUL. Don't press me about this, Berta.
BERTA. You're acting awfully strange, is there something wrong?

PAUL. There's nothing wrong. Now, please, could you just drop it.

BERTA. It just seems strange is all. I mean, you leave a party early, you come over here complaining about how awful it was, but you keep looking out the window anyway. What were you looking for? *(By now, everyone is watching PAUL, who has retreated to the center of the room.)* And why did you interrupt me when I said I saw smoke? And why didn't you call the fire department? I saw you standing there, just holding the phone.

MOLLY. Mom, what the hell are you talking about? What are you saying?

BERTA. I'm concerned, Molly. Jenner, turn on the lights. *(JENNER does not move.)* Did you do something at the party tonight? Did you ...

PAUL. ... Did I what?

BERTA. Where did you leave your cigarette lighter? You told Molly you lost it. Well, where is it?

MOLLY. Mom, you can't be serious.

PAUL. It's okay. *(Slowly PAUL reaches into his pocket and pulls out a cigarette. He twirls it in his hand then sticks it in his mouth. Then he reaches into another pocket and pulls out his lighter. He lights it and watches the flame. Then he lights his cigarette.)* I asked Molly for a light because I was flirting with her. That doesn't make me an arsonist does it?

MOLLY. I thought you were going to give up smoking.

PAUL. I say that every year. So far the record is about an hour.

JENNER. Why don't you just go now.

PAUL. What's wrong, Jenner?

JENNER. I don't like you.

PAUL. Well you have reason enough. Did you really think she'd ever fall for you?

(MOLLY moves to PAUL.)

MOLLY. Please ... leave him alone.

BERTA. Molly, get away from him! He could be dangerous.

MOLLY. Mom, stop! You can't keep doing this to me! You think I don't know why Tom left? You think I don't know about the things you said to him. You keep telling me you want me to be happy, but if I start to be then you try to ruin it.

BERTA. Molly, we don't know him.

PAUL. Now you're getting it. Now you're catching on. You don't know me. None of you know me. I could have burned down that building. Or, I could be a figment of your imaginations. If I walk out of here you're all right back where you started. But I'm not going anywhere. You want to talk about order, Jenner? The only order there is is that the old gets replaced by the new. That's order Jenner, that's progress. When things wear down they have to be replaced. Don't think that this *(Indicating JENNER's tower.)* can save you from progress. That's just hiding from the truth. Everything has it's time and your time is up. *(PAUL smashes the tower to the floor. JENNER screams and attacks PAUL who shoves him to the ground near the booth.)* You could at least handle it gracefully.

(PAUL moves toward JENNER.)

BERTA. You leave him alone! *(To JENNER.)* Baby, come here. Come here and put your head on me. *(BERTA pulls a crying JENNER into the booth with her and rocks him.)* That's right. That's good, yes.

JENNER. He ... He ...

BERTA. Hush, don't think about him. You don't have to leave. You don't have to go anywhere. You stay right here with me. Stay with Mamma.

(Silence except for the sound of fire. BERTA continues to gently rock JENNER. MOLLY is standing in front of the juke

box watching PAUL.)

PAUL. It's ... all right now. Everything's in its proper place. A place for everyone and everyone in their place. *(Pause. To MOLLY.)* Will you dance with me?

(MOLLY considers it then turns to the juke box and selects a sad old song. MOLLY removes her apron then goes to the window and turns around the "Open" sign. Meanwhile, PAUL kicks away some of the broken dishes. They meet center. PAUL takes MOLLY's hand and they dance slowly. Fade out music, lights, and sound of fire.

END OF PLAY

PROPS

Dishes (enough plates, bowls, cups, water glasses, and silverware for four place settings)
Paper place mats
French fries
Tomato rice soup
Club sandwich
Reuben sandwich
Tabloid newspaper
Ice water pitcher
Coffee pot
Rag for Molly
3 Party Hats
3 Party Horns
Purse for Berta
Cigarettes
Cigarette Lighter
3 Ashtrays (for counter, table, booth)
Calendar (preferably something obnoxiously cute)
Christmas garland/other small decorations

A NOTE ON COSTUMES

BERTA should wear clothes appropriate to her age, perhaps a sweater and a long skirt. Festive holiday colors are good.

JENNER should wear his work clothes: an oxford shirt which fits a little too tight, dark pants and dark shoes.

MOLLY should wear a decent white blouse, a skirt, an apron and comfortable shoes. She should *not* wear a waitress uniform.

PAUL should wear a well-tailored dark suit and very attractive, but subdued shoes.

40 SPECKS

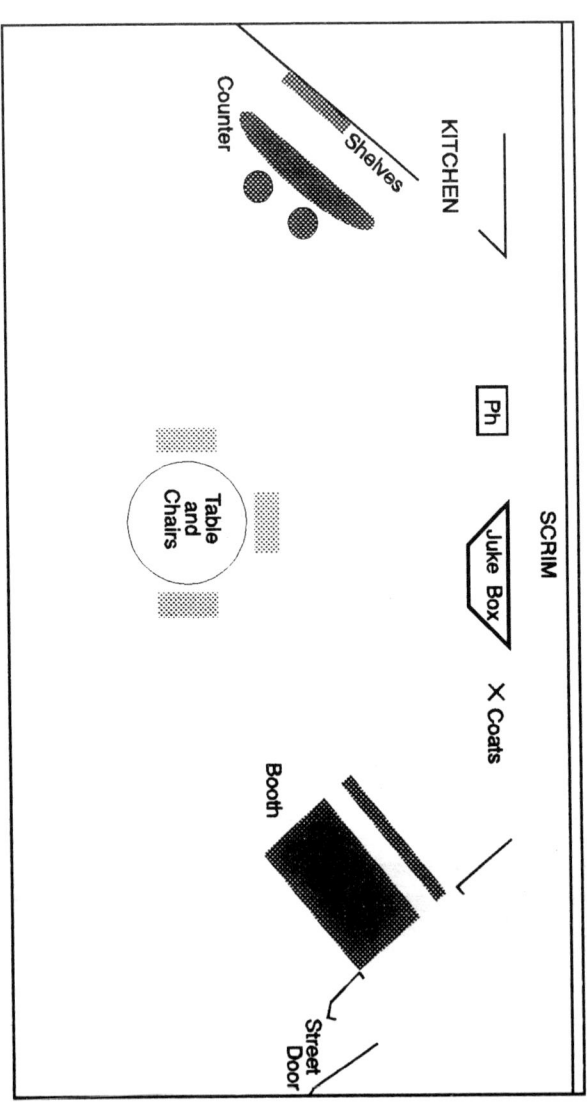

Floor Plan

FAVORITE ONE-ACT PLAYS
from
SAMUEL FRENCH, INC.

THE APOLLO OF BELLAC – ARIA DA CAPO –
THE BALD SOPRANO – BIRDBATH – THE
BROWNING VERSION – CALM DOWN MOTHER –
THE CHAIRS – CHAMBER MUSIC – CHINAMEN –
COMINGS AND GOINGS – COP-OUT – DEATH –
THE FLATTERING WORD – FUNNYHOUSE OF A
NEGRO – THE FUTURE IS IN EGGS – THE
GLOAMING, OH MY DARLING – GOD – THE GOLDEN
FLEECE – HANDS ACROSS THE SEA – THE HAPPY
JOURNEY TO CAMDEN AND TRENTON –
HERE WE ARE – IF MEN PLAYED CARDS AS
WOMEN DO – JACK, OR THE SUBMISSION –
THE LESSON – THE LOVE COURSE – LUNCHTIME –
THE MAN WITH THE FLOWER IN HIS MOUTH –
NOT ENOUGH ROPE – OUT OF OUR FATHER'S
HOUSE – OVERTONES – POOR AUBREY –
THE PRIVATE EAR – THE PROBLEM – THE PUBLIC
EYE – THE RECOGNITION SCENE FROM ANASTASIA
– RED CARNATIONS – RIDERS TO THE SEA –
SCHUBERT'S LAST SERENADE – THE STILL ALARM
– STILL LIFE – THE TWELVEPOUND LOOK –
WHITE LIARS

For descriptions of plays, consult our Basic Catalogue of Plays.

THE SAMUEL FRENCH THEATER BOOKSHOP

Specializing in plays and books on the theater

SAMUEL FRENCH, INC. (New York)
45 West 25th Street
New York, NY 10010-2751
(212) 206-8990 (FAX 212-206-1429)
(open 9:00-5:00, Mon.-Fri.)

SAMUEL FRENCH, INC. (California)
7623 Sunset Blvd   11963 Ventura Blvd.
Hollywood, CA 90046-2795 Studio City, CA 91604
(323) 876-0570   (818) 762-0535
FAX 323-876-6822
(call for hours)

SAMUEL FRENCH, (Canada) LTD.
100 Lombard Street
Toronto, Ontario M5C 1M3
CANADA
(416) 363-3536
(open 9:00-5:00, Mon.-Fri.)

SAMUEL FRENCH LTD. (England)
52 Fitzroy Street
London W1P 6JR
England
(open 9:30-5:30, Mon.-Fri.)

ISBN 0 573 62663 4   # 21436